VENDORLAND

EVENT MARKETING, SIMPLIFIED

GINA VALENTINE

VENDORLAND

Event Marketing, Simplified

ISBN: 978-1-685730-21-5

Faith is taking
the first step,
even when you
don't see the
whole staircase.

—MARTIN LUTHER KING JR.

Contents

Preface

Take a Deep Breath and Exhale!

This book was designed to offer practical support to **the event vendor, the small or large business owner** who is actively participating in events, i.e., activations, trade shows, festivals, VIP events, etc.

My goal is to simply support your efforts and shift your paradigm: You will learn how to create a successful event space just like that of the Fortune 500 brands.

I have extracted and compiled practical tips from twenty-five years of experience just for you, the event vendor.

This practical manual will show you how to:

- Establish and increase brand awareness at an event
- Create an innovative, cohesive event space
- Court, engage, and marry your customer
- Increase foot traffic and product sales (producing measurable results)
- Increase return on investment
- Create loyal consumers

This book will simplify your event vending and grow your business!

Introduction

Let me tell you! I have personally managed and executed every kind of event for nearly three decades.

I fell in love with the world of corporate events during my junior year of college, back in 1996. While finishing my B.A. degree at Columbia College of Chicago, I was awarded an internship in Promotions & Events at a conservative Chicago radio station, WNUA 95.5. It was the smooth jazz station for elite Chicagoans. In this internship, I did everything from cleaning the promotional closet to executing events at the oldest outdoor music festival in the United States, Ravinia (held in Highland Park, Illinois).

After my graduation in June 1997, I did not immediately start out in the corporate promotions and events industry because my goal was monetary, not passion fulfillment. I ended up landing a job as a client manager for Sears Roebuck & Co., servicing clients via direct mail and telemarketing. This mundane desk job, managing spreadsheets and call centers, lasted about six months, before I realized the event world was where I wanted to be.

In 1998, I secured a position as a senior event coordinator at E. Morris Communications, a mid-sized full-run advertising agency servicing Fortune 500 brands like General Motors (Oldsmobile) and Nestle (Ralston Purina Puppy Chow).

On behalf of my client Oldsmobile, we pitched and executed two thirty-city tours (in thirty-one days): a live syndicated radio-remote tour, the *Tom Joyner Morning Show*, and the second tour, Oldsmobile with Iyanla Vanzant meet-and-greet tour. Both tours required multiple qualifications, including but not limited to: teamsmanship, production management, event management, client management, field management, sweepstakes fulfillment, tour management, etc.

By the age of twenty-three, I was living my best life! I had purchased my own one-bedroom condo in the Hyde Park neighborhood of Chicago and found myself living a very glamorous lifestyle. My work life and social life seamlessly merged. In addition to my salary, I was offered many perks, including extensive travel, a private limo driver, a cell phone allowance, a corporate AMEX account, VIP access to events, and frequent meet-and-greets with celebrities.

I never looked back! Corporate events & promotions is where I belong!

In retrospect, working in the events and promotions department for a full-run advertising agency was a privilege. The events department was part of an agency team alongside Account Services, Media, P.R., Sales, Creative, etc. **What differentiates me from any other event professional is that "I understand how events and brand promotions fit into the full scope of a marketing campaign."** I am not your average events person; I am a marketing executive who fell in love with the experiential aspect of marketing! Managing events is just one of many promotional tools used to support a comprehensive marketing strategy. While working in advertising, I also gained invaluable experience working with a team of seasoned professionals, cultivating a strong work ethic and lifelong relationships.

In every chapter of this book, I will use the following systematic outline:

1. Set expectations and talk about the chapter's topic.
2. Offer real-world experience and examples from my portfolio/ experience.
3. Provide the "Nuts & Bolts," offering details and clarity in explaining industry habits/behavior.
4. Summarize the information provided, then follow with a cohesive plan of action.

CHAPTER ONE

Event Marketing 101, Keep It Simple

In the world of marketing and promotions, the term *events* can include, but is not limited to, event activations, tradeshows, expositions, festivals, conferences, art shows, markets, tastings, demos, road shows, runs/walks, galas, in-store demos, block parties, back-to-school events, VIP events, and on-premise and off-premise activations.

Personally, I've executed any and every kind of event on a local and national level. This extensive experience has created the foundation of my career in corporate events and promotions for the past twenty-five years (and counting). One of my personal goals in writing this book is to simplify marketing industry lingo so you can easily enhance your business objectives.

Please feel free to utilize the index for clarity.

IN THIS CHAPTER, WE WILL CLARIFY:

- A footprint
- The importance of an impression
- Why (experiential) event marketing is still relevant in today's digital world

NUTS & BOLTS:

The event space you secure at an event to market your product or service is called a *footprint*. A standard event footprint is usually a 10x10 ft. space.

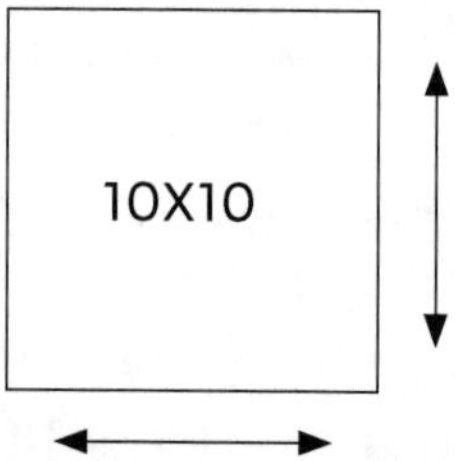

footprint

/'footprint/

noun

noun: **footprint**; the impression left by a foot or shoe on the ground or a surface

synonyms:

footmark, footstep, mark, impression;

When you examine the definition of the word *footprint*, does the word **impression** grab you?

A footprint is a common industry term used to define the (paid) vendor event space. First, you should understand that your event footprint is a critical component of your overall brand's development, sales, growth, and longevity.

Your event footprint makes an impression on every single event attendee.

An event footprint is just one (of many) promotional tools used in a cohesive marketing campaign. Marketers use multiple promotional tools at the same time with the same message to communicate with their customers and/or prospective customers. This process is called an "Integrated Marketing Campaign" (IMC), also known as "the IMC process."

An established event footprint will always:

- ⇨ Command attention.
- ⇨ Set a consistent mood and/or experience.
- ⇨ Evoke an emotional connection with a particular audience consistent across the brand.

> This emotional connection should entice one or all five of the human senses, and consistency is key to the growth and longevity of your brand. You want your footprint to demand interest and leave an impactful impression at every single event.

SIMPLE QUESTIONS TO ASK YOURSELF:

- ? What lasting impression do people have about my brand, product, or service?
- ? What is the current culture, feel, mood, and design (message) of my brand?
- ? Is the overall impression and culture of my footprint cohesive across all my marketing efforts, i.e., social media, website, etc.?
- ? How can I make my brand come alive in my event footprint?

IN SUMMARY

Why is experiential marketing still important in today's digital world? Because human engagement is the most successful form of marketing and promotion, it's called "word of mouth." And I have good news for you! Your event footprint gives you the opportunity to directly (face-to-face) mold and influence people's impressions of your brand, product, or service. You also have the ability to create an emotional connection with every single event attendee and create a long-lasting relationship inside and outside your footprint. The strategy of selling a product or service through experiences that engage customers and create an emotional attachment to the product or service is simply called "experiential marketing."

As with any human relationship, if properly cultivated, an emotional attachment can last forever via word of mouth passed down from generation to generation.

▼ DID YOU KNOW?

Your brand image is "what people feel and say about your brand when you are not around."

CHAPTER TWO

Identify Your TA, Know Your Audience!

In this chapter, you will gain knowledge of how to identify your primary customer and profile your customers' common interests. You will also learn how to apply the five steps of the event footprint to establish brand consistency, which will lay a solid foundation for building an emotional connection.

Most entrepreneurs have an idea of whom they would like to sell their product or service to, but they are actually *not* clear on who their current customer is! You need to know and/or discover your brand's target audience.

A close friend of mine and former agency colleague started her very own cheesecake business in the summer of 2017.

She used her great-aunt's popular cheesecake recipe and launched a vibrant brand concept. She began by launching a website that featured free delivery; in addition, she strategically selected high-traffic local Chicago events that would pair well with her brand and product while giving her an opportunity to sample attendees. I had the privilege of assisting her with some of these trade shows and festivals. After multiple successful events in which the product sold out, she quickly gathered critical sampling feedback and discovered her greatest supporter and/or primary customer was a middle-aged or older Caucasian female.

This niche audience was instinctively drawn to her footprint, easily engaged, willing to sample the product, and ready to buy "Aunt Viola's Cheesecake"! This niche audience was also willing to participate in live video testimonials for social-media engagement and to spread the word.

Overall, the sampling feedback yielded several successes:

* A niche target audience was verified.
* A new product was developed: "moo-moo cheesecake," a five-inch personal size.
* Future events were carefully vetted, selecting (future) tradeshows and festivals with the same niche target audience.

5 STEPS OF THE EVENT FOOTPRINT

Identifying your target audience is the beginning of the five-step customer courting process.

Your event footprint should always:

1. Identify your target audience (TA).
2. Initiate a relationship with your TA.
3. Create an emotional connection with your TA.
4. Meet your TA's expectations.
5. Sustain a long-term relationship with your TA.

When you begin the courting process with your target audience, you have the ability to attract, engage, connect, and marry your customer just like iconic brands do, including Nike, Starbucks, and Amazon. These brands have been able to successfully establish a long-term (brand-loyal) relationship with their TA, and they have made that loyal consumer their greatest promoter.

Companies and businesses spend thousands and even millions of dollars identifying their target audience through extensive market research. This extensive research results in various key learnings, such as: Who is the primary customer? Why do they like the brand? Why do they like the product and service? What are their habits, likes or dislikes, lifestyle, culture, purchase behaviors, etc.? In conclusion, the marketer can easily create a persona for that TA. The marketer will invest all their dollars and efforts to create a strategy to attract, court, engage, and eventually marry this audience!

MARKET A LIFESTYLE TO YOUR AUDIENCE

In the late 1990s, I found my career to be very exciting and fulfilling! I wanted more.

Working at EMC (E. Morris Communications) was glamorous, but I quickly learned there was no room to grow within this conservative agency. The experience I had gained and the connections I had built at EMC were just the tip of the iceberg. At the time, Leo Burnett was managing the "general market" account for General Motors and Oldsmobile, and this yielded a much larger budget with much larger benefits and advantages. I began to search for new options.

Not concerned with titles or roles, I discovered a newer, younger, and trendy lifestyle agency (KBA Marketing). This agency managed a big tobacco account, and I was able to make 75 percent of my full-time salary as a part-time brand ambassador. This hip lifestyle agency was staffed with primarily nightlife industry heavyweights: bar managers, bartenders, former musicians, etc., and it specialized in 'experiential marketing.'

In 1998, I worked on the weekends as a brand ambassador at KBA Marketing, and during the week, I traveled extensively at EMC Touring for the Oldsmobile client. Eventually, a full-time role opened at KBA, and I landed my former manager's role as the Chicago program manager for the RJ Reynolds tobacco account.

The tobacco program's account had three legs: secured bar/nightclub contracts with bar owners to exclusively sell cigarettes and create experiences (events) in the nightclubs; secured contracts with local retail accounts to influence tobacco consumers at the time of purchase; and multiple exclusive event concerts with prominent artists: Oscar award winner Common; Grammy Award winners Teena Marie; and the legendary James Brown.

I vividly remember one of my interview questions: "What are the last three CDs you purchased?" At the time, I thought this was such a strange question for an interview.

I realized KBA Marketing wasn't just pitching a marketing strategy to a client. KBA Marketing knew they had a unique (niche) underground audience, and they were pitching a niche lifestyle. The agency culture was a select group of influencers who inhabited the brand's lifestyle, which gained a favorable response from the client and the brand's target audience. This strategy increased brand awareness and incrementally increased sales.

Brilliant, ABSOLUTELY! I had to be a part of this new movement.

At the time of the writing of this book, I am now entering my seventh semester of lecturing at Columbia College of Chicago, my alma mater. During one of my in-class lecture discussions, the topic was consumer brand loyalty. I asked each student to give me one brand or product they faithfully used, that under no circumstances would they ever switch away from. I vividly remember one of my students explaining why she was loyal to Crest toothpaste. She said that no matter what, she would never purchase any other brand of toothpaste. She explained that her mother purchased Crest toothpaste when she was a child, and currently while she was away at school, Crest toothpaste reminded her of her mother and home.

Wow! Think about how profound that is. A brand can evoke an emotional response and a warm, nostalgic memory in a person. From this conversation, I gathered that Crest toothpaste emotionally symbolized security and trust for this student. And in this particular case, Crest now has a new generation of loyal consumers.

This kind of emotional connection creates a tradition and another loyal consumer. Now she (my student) is a Crest brand ambassador and influencer. Perhaps through this in-class exercise, someone else was influenced via word of mouth to "trust Crest toothpaste"?

To further simplify, one of the fundamental goals of a marketing strategy is to create an emotional connection with the TA. If you are able to make an emotional connection with your TA, you can easily influence, sell, and retain your customer.

ASK YOURSELF

Before you commit to an event, you must know the following about your brand.

Who is:

- ? Your primary customer and financial supporter?
- ? Easily attracted to your product or service?
- ? Excited about your product or service in a positive light?
- ? Freely making referrals without an incentive?

Once you answer these questions, you should find similarities in age, race, ethnicity, and geographic location. If you examine this audience closely, you may be able to identify similar patterns in their lifestyle, behaviors, and culture. It is a very strong possibility that this group of customers is your **current TA**.

CHAPTER THREE

Initiate a Relationship, Set the Mood

Set the mood, send a message, and let the courtship begin!

As with any road toward marriage, the process of courtship should involve "intentional moments of engagement."

Now that you understand that your event space is an actual footprint at an event, you should want to leave an impression strategically in pursuit of your TA.

I would like to shift your paradigm and challenge you to view your footprint as a vortex, a new world that offers niche experiences. Your footprint is an entrance into your brand's world and establishes your brand's authenticity. Like a human footprint, no one else has the same DNA or structure. Yes, this may sound magical or dramatic, but this is what successful event activation is all about!

Let's try a simple exercise: If you close your eyes and think about the word *Candyland*, what does your imagination create? I can guarantee a definite color palette, feeling, and smell of this fictitious place. I guarantee that my imaginary Candyland is different from your imaginary Candyland based on our age, race, ethnicity, culture, etc. But there will also be commonalities in our expectations; what we create in our imaginations will be based on similar expectations. For example, we both expect A LOT OF CANDY. It's Candyland!

What your imagination has created is called a "MOOD."

One part of a marketing strategy is creating a mood board to entice, engage, and meet the TA's expectations.

If you were creating a Candyland event footprint, the design layout would be based on your TA.

Let's say your TA was a Baby Boomer, born between the early to mid-1940s and 1964.

The color palette of your Candyland footprint would mirror the Baby Boomers' childhood period, i.e., the 1950s. We could expect to see brands of candy reflecting that period: Atomic Fireballs, Charleston Chews, Orange Slices, etc. Your staff may be dressed in fifties' outfits, and there may be music playing from artists like Elvis, Chuck Berry, Ray Charles, Little Richard, and Johnny Cash.

Marketers depend on "setting a mood" for a brand. They are the temperature setters for how they want their TA to view their product or service.

You are in control of your event space, and your event space should have a set mood but also meet some or all of your TA's expectations. This mood should align with all of your business components (social media, website, logo, etc.) and be consistent.

Consistency is **critical** in making a lasting impression on your customers.

Now you are ready to create a mood board (a digital mood board is an option).

MOOD BOARD

The objective of the mood board is to ENTICE & ENGAGE THE EMOTIONS OF YOUR TA (ONLY).

For the mood board, simply gather relevant images for your brand and establish a cohesive and consistent emotion. I strongly advise that you begin with your brand logo and keep every image in alignment with that logo: color, font, style, etc. Make sure you create a cohesive mood for your footprint, i.e., a welcoming haven, a wild adventure, or an indigenous ritual.

HOW BIG BRANDS DO IT

Think of a big brand like McDonald's or Subway. Every store has a consistent mood in any location, no matter what city you visit. The signage, logo, colors, feel, and smell of the location are consistent with the overall brand image. Consistency **creates a brand identity and a key message** that make a connection with the TA and meet the customers' expectations. These factors ultimately create a long-term relationship with the customer and promote repeat purchases, creating what is called a "loyal consumer."

For example, a PepsiCo brand, IZZE Sparkling Fruit Juice, was my client for over five years, and the brand message was simply "100% fruit juice mixed with sparkling water, a healthy alternative to soda."

In 2009, at Whole Foods stores, we created a visual display to reinforce that message with glass pitchers of artificial fruit that mirrored the product flavors we were sampling.

At the annual 2010 PepsiCo sales meeting, my team visually represented the IZZE brand message by partnering with a culinary chef to create large, dramatic vases filled with chopped fresh fruit immersed in carbonated water. This was a great visual image since the fruit directly reflected the flavors of the product: apple, blackberry, grapefruit, etc.

What was the message (impression) for the TA?

* Pure fruit juice and sparkling water
* Healthy alternative to soda
* Refreshing
* Light
* Fun
* Colorful

Successful impressions invoke feelings! When our feelings are stimulated, it helps create an emotional connection.

In 2009, I was a newly single mother seeking local work that did not require extensive travel. I was able to secure a marketing manager position with an experiential agency in Boulder, Colorado, for a PepsiCo brand, IZZE Sparkling Fruit Juice. The target audience was females between the ages of twenty-one and thirty-four. This product was such a refreshing brand to represent. Not only was I a mom in my mid-thirties myself, but I was living a holistic lifestyle, and IZZE was my personal beverage of choice! I was personally the target audience, authentically promoting a lifestyle as a "healthy alternative to soda."

I had the opportunity to represent IZZE Sparkling Fruit Juice from 2009 to 2015, both locally and nationally. The program shifted seasonally: small events with thirty to fifty thousand attendees, VIP events co-partnering with brands like Crate & Barrel and Lululemon, and finally, festivals like Chipotle Cultivate Festivals and Bon Appetite in Millennium Park, Chicago. I also supported the PepsiCo sales teams with annual trade show conventions and VIP mixers.

Every program challenged me to innovate!

At times, I hired interior designers, florists, chefs, artists, etc., to assist with producing various event footprints. Each footprint was uniquely designed to engage the brand's TA and the event attendees. Every footprint had a consistent message: "Real fruit juice mixed with sparkling water." The brand's personality was light, fun, and healthy.

In an effort to be alluring and connect with the brand's target audience, we created unique, consistent brand experiences at every event, communicating the same brand message to the target audience: a "healthy alternative to soda."

> In 2010, at the McCormick Place sales meeting, the IZZE lounge was filled with multicolored gerbera daisies (representing the product variety of flavors), branded bicycle, sofa, highboy/chairs, IZZE branded art, branded pillows, and ice-cold IZZE limited new flavors (samples).

> At the 2010 Crate & Barrel Bridal Brunch, we merged décor and mimosas, showing that IZZE is a great mixer! The (orange) clementine mixed very well with champagne while couples perused the store and created their bridal registry.

> In 2011, the BlogHER conference culinary chef displayed multiple glass pitchers with fresh-cut fruit submerged in sparkling water, i.e., flavors of blackberry, pomegranate, grapefruit, clementine, etc.

> In 2012, at the Chipotle Cultivate Festival, we discovered one of the brand's flavors, clementine (seedless tangerine), was foreign. People were unsure exactly what a clementine was, so we created a "clementine peeling contest," and the winners received branded swag.

> At the 2018 Bon Appetit Festival, we debuted a new partnership with Chipotle, creating a log cabin with Chipotle burritos and ice-cold IZZE Sparkling Fruit Juice. We created a second footprint in the VIP room, where top chefs were preparing hot meals with IZZE served as a cocktail mixer.

The objective of every footprint experience should be to create a consistent brand message.

Think: Where is "the happiest place on earth"?

Yes, DISNEY WORLD!

This is their brand message.

NUTS & BOLTS

Differentiation is key to sustaining a competitive advantage.

Your footprint should educate your TA on your unique niche.

While you innovate exciting experiences, you also want to communicate the value of your product or service.

So, tell me, if you are selling lemonade, what's different about it? Is it sweetened with agave nectar, which offers a low-glycemic sweetening factor and caters to the diabetic audience? Does it have gummy bears at the bottom of every serving and excite children between the ages of three and fifteen? Is the packaging unique, i.e., an innovative thermal bottle that stays ice cold for up to seventy-two hours, which attracts campers or farmers?

In summary, make sure the value is clearly communicated through the brand message and overall experience.

ASK YOURSELF

? What is my brand message, and how can I connect that message with my TA?

? How can I make my product or service come alive at the event?

? How can I create an event within an event?

? How can I execute this experience?

? How can I ensure that my target audience is overwhelmingly engaged by this brand experience?

IN SUMMARY

> Everyone has a story; tell your story.

> What is the narrative of your brand?

> **Your brand story should be engaging, informative, educational, and unique!**

> Your story needs to be original, influential, and concise.

> Keep it simple!

CHAPTER FOUR

Designing the Footprint, Make a Bold Statement

Let's now design the footprint and make a bold impression!

There are two important aspects when designing your footprint:

1. The design logistics: structure, layout, specs
2. The footprint personality, which entices the five senses

DESIGN LOGISTICS

Create a visual layout of how you will display your event materials. I encourage you to take the extra step and map out a mock visual of your footprint. This can be a photo, a digital image, or a simple drawing.

It doesn't have to be fancy; it just has to be practical.

What are your designated event spaces (measurements): 10x10, 20x20? Is this an indoor or an outdoor event? For an outdoor event, perhaps you need a 10x10 tent with sandbags. Is this an indoor corner footprint in which you need two 8-foot tables with tablecloths? All the event materials need to be intentional and assembled.

I suggest creating a list of event materials for proper preparation: i.e., tent, table, signage, pamphlets, products, stanchions, tablecloths, area rugs, fresh flowers, etc.

You should also include an activation kit with self-help items: i.e., Band-Aids, Benadryl tablets, bottled water, tape, measuring tape, permanent markers, string, safety pins, rubber bands, FedEx mailing labels, paper towels, Clorox wipes, garbage cans, trash bags and liners, recycle bins, and *this book*! Smiles.

Perhaps you have a last-minute emergency or are starting to get an awful cold on the day of the event. The show must go on! These items will be extremely helpful to your replacement.

QUESTIONS TO ASK YOURSELF:

Is the footprint:

? Consistent with the product or service branding—mood?

? Clearly conveying the brand message?

? Fluid, comfortable, friendly, interactive, and engaging?

? Weatherized?

? Geometrically balanced? Promoting feng shui?

? Inviting? Ideally, you would like for people to engage with your brand.

? Organized and safe, including for children, pets, the handicapped, etc.

? Interactive for all ages, all event attendees?

*Not artistically inclined? Just use a ruler and create some simple rectangles, or even draw circles or stick figures; it does not have to be fancy. You want to map out images that represent your brand. Simply emulate this feeling within your footprint.

THE FIVE SENSES OF THE DESIGN

I am a firm believer in using the strategy of engaging all five senses. When you target your audience's five senses, you will make a successful impact that builds a long-term emotional connection.

The five senses include sight, touch, smell, sound, and taste.

Did you know you can create multiple levels of impressions at every event you attend? Set the temperature. Create the mood and influence not only the people who visit your footprint, but everyone who is a part of the event! Seize the power!

SIGHT: The brand design should be visible and consistent.

Signage! Signage! Signage! You would not believe how many vendors do not have enough substantial signage in their footprint. Your brand logo should be anywhere and everywhere you can place it without compromising the brand's integrity (making it look cheap or cheesy). On the tent top, the walls, a table runner, a static foot decal, individual price tags, QR codes, etc. Remember: This is a brand experience; visitors should never leave your footprint without being impacted.

Where can the TA find your product or service after the event? Signage should always be simple but detailed. For example, display the brand logo with the website address, QR codes, social media handles, and/or the brick-and-mortar address.

TOUCH: Give them something to touch, to interact with!

How does your brand *feel*? The feeling of the brand must align with your brand message. If you are selling a product, you must allow people to feel, touch, smell, and interact with the product. Always include a demonstration, if possible.

SMELL: Smells can either attract or deter!

What does your brand smell like? This is one of the most challenging senses to entice due to vendor guidelines; however, it is possible. Think about nature. What does nature smell like? Aside from candles, think about using spices, essential oils, flowers, coffee beans, etc. to affect the sensory response of smell in your TA.

SOUND: Sound travels.

What does your brand sound like? Sound can be stimulated through games, prizes, chants, music, tranquil waterfalls, drums, live musicians, guest speakers, etc. However, these sounds should always align with your brand message and appeal to your TA. If you are selling international goods, using world music should be a given!

TASTE: Sample or initiate a pairing.

Obviously, if you are selling an edible product, you should engage consumers with complimentary samples. What if you are selling an item that is not edible? Conduct a pairing! For example, if you are selling abstract art at a summer expo, serve complimentary wine! *Acquiring a liquor sponsorship is another option.

"Word of mouth" is the most effective form of promotion.

You want people to share your brand!

BUILD EXCITEMENT

Use the following to build excitement at your footprint around your brand.

- ✳ GAMES
- ✳ CONTESTS
- ✳ INCENTIVES (free swag, branded valuable Items)

* GUEST SPEAKER (subject matter expert, industry guru)
* INFLUENCERS
* ENTERTAINMENT (DJ, singer, musician, artist)
* ARTS/CRAFTS
* SELFIE STATION (360 Experience, etc.)

Over time, executing eight to twelve events a week for PepsiCo/IZZE Sparkling Fruit Juice, clementine became one of IZZE Sparkling Fruit Juice's top four flavors, and people were always asking about it. We discovered from actual customer feedback that people did not know what a clementine was. With our TA at the forefront of our minds (females between the ages of twenty-one and thirty-four), in 2009, at the Chipotle Cultivate Festival in Chicago (30K attendees), we decided to order five hundred clementines and create a "clementine peeling contest." The winners received branded free premiums: T-shirts, free products, and clementine-flavored IZZE lip balm.

Not only did this promotional strategy engage our current loyal customers and entice new prospective customers, but it also created great excitement in our footprint and resulted in long lines for participation. The "clementine peeling contest" educated our attendees regarding the product while fulfilling the brand message, and it was very successful!

NUTS & BOLTS

- ⇨ Professionals pay attention to details.
- ⇨ Give your footprint a personality!
- ⇨ Make discoveries and brainstorm solutions.
- ⇨ Take notes and recap your event footprints over time. Assess what works and what doesn't, then rinse and repeat!

In conclusion, through your footprint, you are connecting and creating an invaluable, memorable experience!

CHAPTER FIVE

A Pivotal Walk-Through, Preparation Promotes Good Success

Preparation promotes good success; get a preview before the event.

When booking your event space, ask permission to see the space; this is called an "event walk-through." All event vendors visit their event spaces one to seven days before the actual event.

If there is no set walk-through time, you can request an appointment. This walk-through can take anywhere from ten minutes to one hour. It depends on the size of the event. The walk-through can also take place during the load-in time. However, if the load-in day is the same as the event, you will want to preview the secured footprint before the designated load-in time. Remember, you are the vendor or customer, and you are paying for the space. You should always be able to see what you are paying for.

To prepare for the walk-through, bring the event map, mood board, a footprint layout, a camera, a pen and paper, and measuring tape. You should easily be able to assess whether your vision (footprint layout) is doable and make the necessary adjustments.

You also want to map out the following within the overall event space:

* Elevators/stairs
* Fire exits
* Restrooms
* Garbage cans/recycle bins
* Registration area
* Security
* Ice machine (if applicable)
* Additional storage (if applicable)
* Medical help/Red Cross station (common for festivals)

- VIP lounges (if accessible in your vendor package)
- Food/beverage stations

You want to be fully equipped to serve the event attendees, fellow vendors, and staff.

You will become a **valuable vendor**, and this is a key advantage!

ADDITIONAL OBSERVATIONS

You should also identify the following:

Direct & Indirect Competitors: other vendors with similar products or services, which can ultimately decrease your ROI.

Let's say you are selling delicious lemonade at this event, but on the day of your walk-through, you discover the event coordinator has secured a total of five beverage vendors, three of whom are neighbors. This would be a disaster for your footprint because it is very unlikely that event attendees would sample and/or purchase all three beverages. This would be a great opportunity for you to contact your event coordinator and renegotiate your footprint location.

Complimentary Vendors: vendors with whom you can partner (directly or indirectly) to increase sales.

These vendors can help you increase your sales as you strategically connect with them and build an alliance! For example, let's say there are five beverage vendors, and you are one of them. You could source a food vendor selling an edible product that "pairs" well with your lemonade and cross-promote with this vendor. The easiest way to initiate that relationship is to offer that vendor a free sample of your product. You never know how successful this could be! That vendor may agree to: send foot traffic to your footprint, hand out branded information about your product, or display your product as their paired preferred beverage! Ultimately, you are creating a free brand ambassador among your colleagues and increasing your sales.

CHAPTER SIX

Conquering the Event Environment, Create a Buzz

Congratulations! You have created an exciting, interactive footprint.

At this stage, you have:

* Secured your event space.
* Identified your TA.
* Created a mood board and footprint layout.
* Completed a walk-through.
* Completed extensive research on the event and the event theme/industry.
* This chapter is about relationships. Period.

Now Let's Create a Buzz...

- Storytelling and repeat brand messaging should be part of the footprint atmosphere.
- Only your brand should be visible within your footprint. If you are selling jewelry, all the staff in your footprint should be wearing that jewelry exclusively. Period.

Every relationship should be viewed as an opportunity, and no relationship should be discounted. Do your best to network and connect with everyone. Yes, everyone! This includes the event manager, the janitor, the elevator operator, security, your fellow vendors, and the event attendees.

Not all gossip is bad gossip. You want to engage with everyone and get anyone and everyone to discuss your brand in a positive light at the event. You might call this gossip, but marketers call it "BUZZ."

"WORD OF MOUTH" IS YOUR MOST COST-EFFICIENT MARKETING TOOL!

Empower local event brand ambassadors!

Do not limit your product or service to just event attendees. Some of my best new customers came through "word of mouth." Word of mouth takes place when someone is connected to your brand, product, or service and is motivated to promote it for free! Get to know your fellow vendor neighbor(s). Yes, other vendors can help increase your sales! Do you want your fellow vendors and other vendors to have a positive engagement with you, your brand, and your footprint?

I never discount anyone; everyone is a potential customer or a potential free brand ambassador. One time, we engaged and sampled the garbage collector, and he talked about the product during his entire shift! Everyone at the event is a potential customer, even vendors whom you might consider competitors. The real question is, How well can you connect with people?

The *free* brand ambassador (BA) drives traffic to your business, and everyone is a potential BA.

SUMMARY

Smile. Be prepared. Be friendly. Add value. Be memorable.

CHAPTER SEVEN

Execution with Excellence, Exceed Their Expectations

EVENT FOOTPRINT IMPRESSIONS

Marketing impressions are a common and important field staff reporting metric in the event industry. Event marketing impressions are essentially how many individuals saw your brand's advertising at an event. There are multiple channels from which you can measure event marketing impressions. The more you can categorize the number of impressions collected, the more accurately you can determine the ROI (return on investment) for the advertising.

* From Afar: Yes, there will be people who did not actually visit your footprint, but

they likely developed an impression of your brand from afar: through advertisements, word of mouth, social media, etc. How many people viewed your footprint—from a distance, an aerial view, in the exhibitor catalog, on someone wearing a T-shirt with your logo, someone holding your product—and formed an opinion?

* Walked Past: How many people walked past your footprint and formed a solid opinion of your brand?
* Visited Your Footprint: How many people actually explored your footprint—entered the space, engaged with your staff, purchased a product/service, and developed an opinion?

NUTS & BOLTS

Here are some practical execution tactics:

⇨ Engage in a conversation and be well-versed in your TA's typical activities and hobbies.

⇨ Educate your TA on how to "continue the courtship" and drive traffic to your website or store.

⇨ Incentivize interactive social-media engagement! Use QR codes.

⇨ Brand your event guests and offer a free branded premium (in alignment with your brand message).

IN SUMMARY

The ability to calculate all three of these types of impressions allows you to determine which form of advertising provided the highest return on the dollar. If event impressions generated the highest value per impression, that might suggest adding more on-site advertising at events the following year. If the highest value came from word of mouth, it might be worthwhile to invest in more staffing to increase consumer interactions. The most valuable part of this measurement effort is providing brand teams with an action plan for future activations.

Strategically engage and target all impressions.

Leave no rock unturned.

"An event isn't over until the attendee stops talking about it!"

HELPFUL TIPS

1. When you are strategic about creating a mood at an event footprint, you can easily connect with your TA.
2. Do a little more research about the event before the event! Gathering event details, like the event's origin, mission, history, headliners, etc., is a great way to build excitement for yourself and your event team. This information can also serve you well by creating relationships with your event contacts, fellow vendors, and customers.
3. If you can create a cohesive brand marketing strategy across your mood board (brand personality), brand message, and a unique, compelling story that ties it all together, you will really win!
4. Your event footprint should be consistent, the same, or at least have similar attributes at every single event!
5. Every event has unpredictable fires; good event preparation is key!
6. Details are critical in the event world, and preparation is key, so you can adapt

and make last-minute changes if necessary. Event professionals never attend an event without a cohesive plan.

7. Initiate a conversation about the event's history or offer to share your VIP badge so your neighbor can enjoy refreshments! There is power in numbers, and everyone is there to succeed.
8. Your footprint location is very important! Building a strong relationship with your event contact will definitely work to your advantage. A thrifty way to create a relationship with the event staff and coordinator is to deliver a care package: a thank-you card, sweets, a sample product, or brand-free premiums.
9. Strategically create such a "buzz" around the event that your footprint becomes "the Footprint" to experience. This will also increase your online foot traffic and social media engagement.
10. Set the vendor standard: be exciting and original, and always create a BUZZZZZZZZZ!

Glossary

Baby Boomer	This is the demographic cohort following the Silent Generation and preceding Generation X. There are various timelines defining the start and end of this cohort; demographers and researchers typically use birth years from the early to mid-1940s and ending anywhere from 1960 to 1964.
Brand	Unique design, sign, symbol, word, or a combination of these are employed in creating an image that identifies a product and differentiates it from its competitors. Over time, this image becomes associated with a feeling of credibility, quality, and satisfaction in the consumer's mind.
Brand Ambassador	A person hired by an organization or company to represent a brand in a positive light and, by doing

	so, helps to increase brand awareness and sales.
Brand Authenticity	The extent to which consumers perceive a brand to be consistent, true to its consumers, motivated by caring and responsibility, and able to support consumers in being true to themselves.
Brand Loyalty	A positive feeling toward a brand and dedication to purchase the same product or service repeatedly now and in the future from the same brand, regardless of a competitor's actions or changes in the environment.
Brand Messaging	The underlying value proposition conveyed and the language used in your content. It's what makes buyers relate to your brand by inspiring, persuading, motivating, and ultimately

	making them want to buy your product.
Customer Loyalty	An attitude and behavioral tendency to favor one brand over all others, whether due to satisfaction with the product or service, its convenience or performance, or simply familiarity and comfort with the brand.
Direct Competitor	A term that describes a company that produces a virtually identical good or service that is offered for sale within the same market.
Impression	An effect, feeling, or image retained resulting from an experience.
Market Research	The process of gathering, analyzing, and interpreting information about a market, a product, or a service to be offered for sale in that market and about the past, present, and potential

	customers for the product or service; research into the characteristics, spending habits, location, and needs of your business's target market, the industry as a whole, and the top competitors.
Marketing Strategy	An organization's strategy that combines all of its marketing goals into one comprehensive plan. A good marketing strategy should be developed based on market research and focus on the right product mix to achieve maximum profit potential and sustain the business.
Mood Board	A mood board is a type of collage consisting of images, text, and samples of objects in a composition. It can be based on a set topic or any material chosen randomly. A mood board can be used to present the general idea

	of a topic or to demonstrate the unique characteristics of a brand or product and how it differs from the competition.
Niche Marketing	Concentrating all marketing efforts on a small but specific and well-defined segment of the population. Niches do not "exist" but are "created" by identifying needs, wants, and requirements that other firms address poorly or not at all and developing and delivering goods or services to satisfy them. As a strategy, niche marketing is aimed at being a big fish in a small pond instead of a small fish in a big pond. It is also called micromarketing.
Persona	In marketing, this is also called a "user persona," "customer persona," or "buyer persona," which is a fictional character

created to represent a user type that might use a site, brand, or product in a similar way. Marketers may use personas together with *market segmentation*, in which the qualitative personas are constructed to be representative of specific segments.

Free Premium — Also known as *swag*! These branded giveaways, i.e., T-shirts, stickers, and water bottles, are the free items given to event attendees and/or customers. The objective of these free premiums is to reward loyal customers, increase brand awareness, and make brands more user-friendly.

Promotion — In marketing, promotion refers to any type of *marketing communication* used to inform or persuade target audiences of the relative merits of a product,

	service, brand, or issue. The aim of promotion is to increase awareness, create interest, generate sales, or create *brand loyalty*. It is one of the basic elements of the *marketing mix*, which includes the four *P*s: price, product, promotion, and place.
Storytelling	This is one of the most powerful ways to breathe life into your brand and is often called one of the main components of a content marketing approach. A brand is a matter of perception. When you tell a story that embodies human challenges, you create an experience that resonates with your customers.
Target Audience	In *marketing* and *advertising*, this is a particular group of *consumers* within a predetermined *target market* identified as the

	targets or recipients of a particular advertisement or message.
ROI	This means *Return on Investment*. It is the ratio between the net profit and cost of investment resulting from an investment in resources.
Word of Mouth	Oral written recommendation by a satisfied customer to prospective customer of a good or service. It's considered to be the most effective form of promotion; it is also called word-of-mouth advertising, which is incorrect because, by definition, advertising is a paid and nonpersonal communication.

Dedication

In 2018, I realized that my career experiences are critical "key learnings" I can share to help others. With my SIMPLISTIC STEPS SERIES, I would like to simplify current marketing challenges that you may face in the business world.

I want to thank Jesus, my Lord and Savior, who has taken me through tremendous valleys and placed all gifts within reach that pertain to life and godliness. Thank you to my strong support system: my father and mother, Ronald and Diane Valentine; my aunt, Doris Smith; my brothers, David and Steven Valentine; my beautiful nieces, Sydney, and Symone Valentine; and my heart—my daughter, Gia N. Crawley. Thank you to my friends who have seen value in me when I could not: Mye Alexis, George Toney III, Tony Bowers, Kamilah and Kabria Cummings, Chamille Weddington, Tina Hernandez, and Ms. Belinda Proctor. I want to thank Mrs. Lillian Neff, who transcended in 2014: thank you for being my ninety-three-year-old best friend. Also, Gregory and Deverieux Tate, Lester Smith, Opal Easter, Michael Ferguson, and Ellyn Hershman, I will never forget how you carried me in my youth. Thank you. Ethel Marcus and Cynthia Cooper, thank you for your endless intercession and encouragement. I am forever grateful, and this is just the beginning of greatness! More greatness is to come!

About the Author

Gina Valentine is a Chicago native who graduated from Columbia College in Chicago with a BA in marketing.

Currently specializing in experiential and entertainment marketing, Gina is a well-seasoned professional with over twenty-five years of marketing experience. In addition to numerous corporate promotional contract positions, she has worked with several full-service advertising agencies.

Most recently, Gina has completed event production freelance projects with clients such as J.P. Morgan Chase, featuring Jamie Dimon and Joe Jonas; the Google Executive Sofi Dinner (undisclosed); a Bill Gates nonprofit organization; and the 2022 64th Annual Grammy Awards.

Currently, she is an adjunct lecturer in the Business and Entrepreneurship Department at Columbia College in Chicago since 2016. Gina has lectured in multiple marketing courses (100–300 level), including Intro to Marketing, Promotional Marketing, Entertainment Marketing, and Developing a Marketing Strategy.

One of her favorite clients/projects was from 2009–2015 at PepsiCo, where she completed five contracts with MatchMG as the local marketing manager for the Chicago IZZE Sparkling Juice program while sourcing and sponsoring key event partners. Gina's local team launched the 2015 "Wholesome Wave" social media campaign on Channel 7 News with Oscar-award winner Common. She was a national marketing manager for the client PepsiCo and IZZE Sparkling Fruit Juice brand for the Chipotle Cultivate festival(s), which attracted over sixty thousand attendees.

Gina is a dedicated mother committed to a holistic lifestyle, a philanthropist, and a community leader. She also enjoys cooking and eating authentic, healthy, and fresh food. Another great passion of hers is traveling; in her leisure time, you will find her biking on Chicago's very own lakefront.

CLIENT LIST INCLUDES:

Allstate Insurance • Amazon • Bacardi • Bai Drinks • Bill Gates Foundation • BNP Media Events • BRAVO Network • Brown-Forman Beverages • Brown & Williamson Tobacco • Chivas • City Colleges of Chicago • Chipotle Cultivate Festivals • Cingular Wireless • CITIBANK • ComEd • CRUNCH Fitness • Curion Insights • Disney • Dream Big Performing

Workshop • DuCAP • eFive • Frontier Snacks • General Motors • 64th Grammy Awards • G.R. N'Namdi Gallery • Herby Pop • Illinois Lottery • IMAX Theatre • IZZE Beverages • KIND BAR • Kraft • Miller Brewing Company • Martell • J.P. Morgan Chase • Naked Juice • Nestle • PEPSICO • Phillips Sonicare • Ralston Purina • Red Bull • R.J. Reynolds • Saturn • Schieffelin & Somerset • Seagrams Co. Ltd. • Sears & Roebucks, Inc. • Soul Beach Music Festival • STAPLES • SunCruz Casinos • TRUTH 2001 Tour • Washington Mutual Bank • WNUA 95.5

Website: www.simplisticstepsseries.com
Instagram: simplisticstepsseries
LinkedIn: www.linkedin.com/in/ginavalentine/